Senior Editor Jane Yorke
Art Editor Toni Rann
Designer Jane Coney
Editorial Director Sue Unstead
Art Director Colin Walton
Photography Stephen Oliver
Additional photography Jane Burton, Peter Chadwick,
Michael Dunning, Dave King, Karl Shone
Hand Models Natalie Davidson, Rachael Legemah
Series Consultant Neil Morris

This is a Dorling Kindersley Book
published by Random House, Inc.

First American edition, 1990

Library of Congress Cataloging-in-Publication Data
My first look at touch.
     p. cm.
   Summary: Text and photos depict the sense of touch,
including things wet, rough, smooth, prickly, squishy, and sticky.
   ISBN 0-679-80623-7
   1.Touch – Juvenile literature. [1. Touch. 2. Senses
and sensation] I. Random House (Firm)
QP451.M9 1990
612.8'8
89-63095 CIP AC

Manufactured in Italy 1 2 3 4 5 6 7 8 9 10

Phototypeset by Flairplan Phototypesetting Ltd, Ware, Hertfordshire
Reproduced in Hong Kong by Bright Arts
Printed in Italy by L.E.G.O.

· MY · FIRST · LOOK · AT ·

Touch

Random House   New York

Wet

ice cubes

seaweed

swimsuit

boat

soap

umbrella

drink

handprint

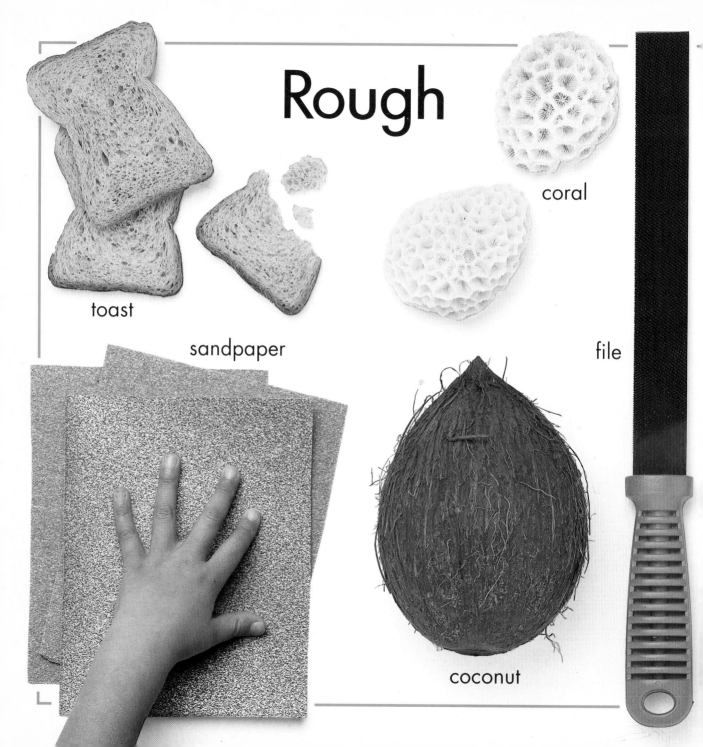

Rough

toast

sandpaper

coral

file

coconut

bark

coasters

pine cones

straw bag

pineapple

Soft

cotton balls

powder puff

yarn

scarf

duck

dandelion

feathers

blanket

Smooth

shell

eggs

geode

marbles

paper

ball

blocks

ribbon

glass

stones

Furry

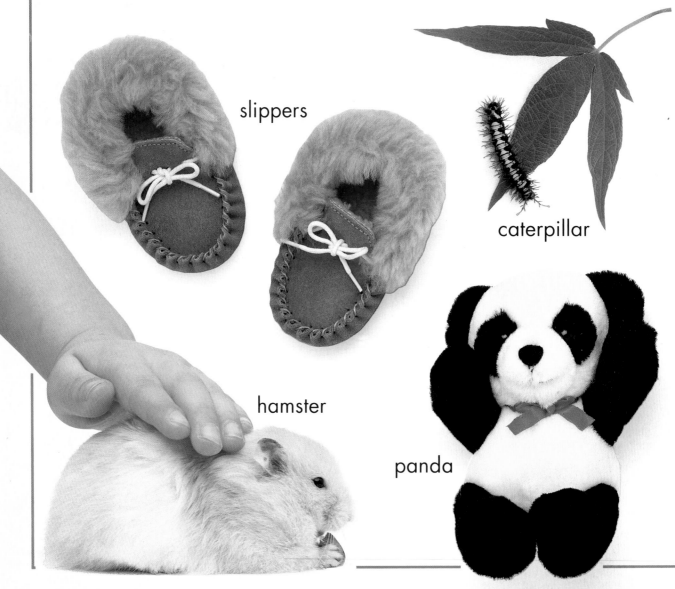

slippers

caterpillar

hamster

panda

beard

winter coat

rabbit

mittens

Prickly

shell

chestnut
bur

roses

holly

pine branch

teasels

bramble

hedgehog

cactus

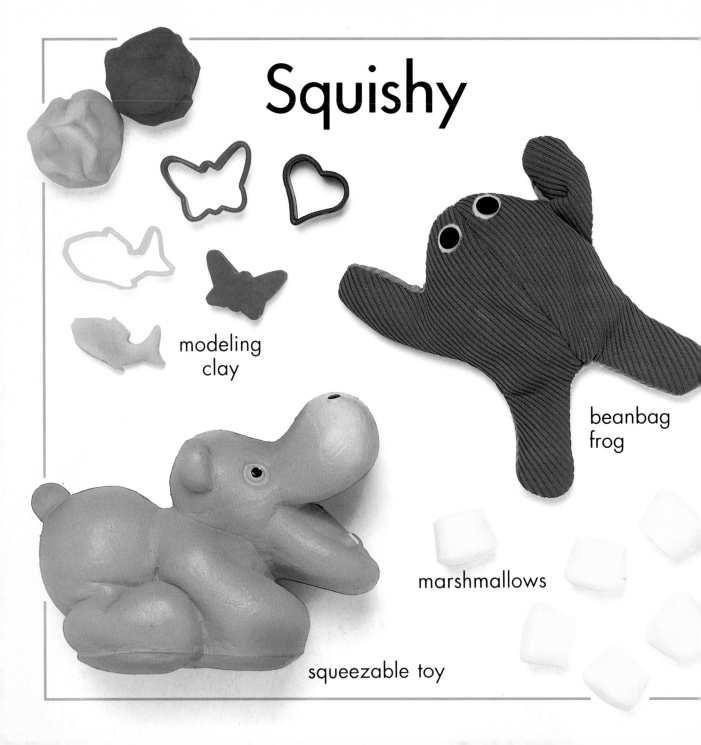

Squishy

modeling clay

beanbag frog

marshmallows

squeezable toy

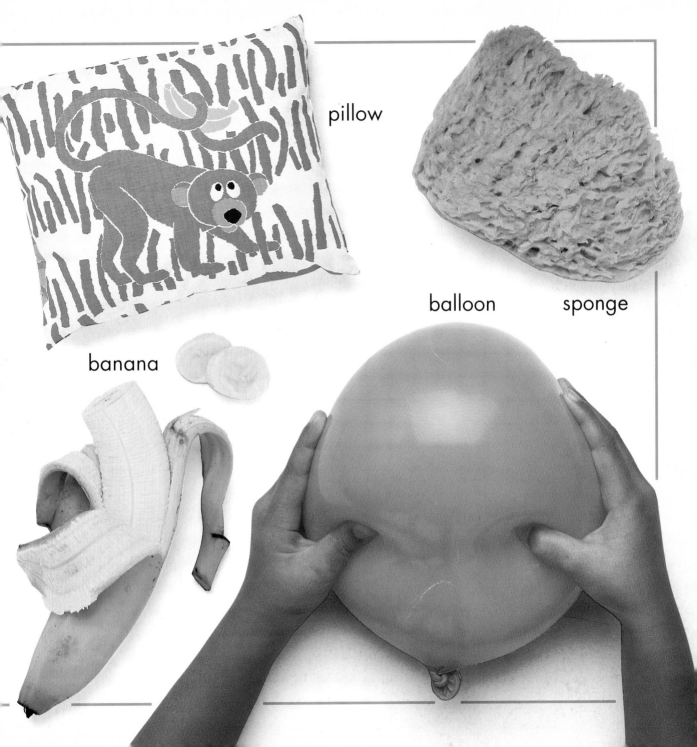

pillow

sponge

balloon

banana

Sticky

taffy

bandages

lollipop

tape

bun

stickers

jam

glue